Suitcase

How To Dump Your Girlfriend

By Julian Daniel & Henry Pumpkin

ISBN 978-1-905778-04-1

www.shorelines.org.uk
admin@shorelines.org.uk

Suitcase books are distributed by Turnaround Publisher Services
Ltd, Unit 3, Olympia Trading Estate, Coburg Rd, Wood Green,
London N22 6TZ.

Illustrations by Paul Neads, www.mucusart.co.uk
design:ianbobb:07799137492:www.axtb.co.uk

Printed by LPPS Ltd,
128 Northampton Rd, Wellingborough, NN8 3PJ

British Library Cataloguing-in-Publication Data. A catalogue record
for this book is available from the British Library.

How To Dump Your Girlfriend

Disclaimer

The publishers and authors disclaim any liability whatsoever from any adverse emotional or physical consequences that may arise from reading this book and acting upon the information contained within.

The advice contained herein is tongue-in-cheek and general in nature. You should always consult experts and professionals from the relationship and/or legal industries before responding in any way when faced with your own particular dilemma. Furthermore, we do not recommend doing anything whatsoever that is not an act between consenting adults and within the laws of England.

Contents

INTRODUCTION

How to dump your girlfriend is a dilemma all ordinary blokes face from time to time. Henry VIII had no trouble dumping his women, it was simply off with their heads, a sprig of parsley to clean the breath then on to test the bedsprings with the next fair maiden. There is part of every man's soul that envies Henry his royal solution.

And of course modern day royalty - that is celebrities - can dump in a style that is great entertainment but not totally useful as a model for ordinary folk. We don't all have the St Tropez hideaway, the helicopter pad for fast flight and the bodyguards for when the plates start flying.

So we have taken it upon ourselves to do a service for ordinary men and put this guide together. Much of our research has been road tested by us through our own experiences with girlfriends. Some of it has come in through friends. We have also done extensive research at bars, clubs, football terraces, chat rooms, speed dating evenings and around the edges of dance floors. The rest we made up.

It boils down to this: dumping your girlfriend is a difficult decision and requires careful thought and planning. You have to be sure you want to dump the girl in the first place. There is no such thing as *the perfect girlfriend*. The 'PG' is a myth put out by marketing people to get us to buy after shave, barbecue grills, new cars and joint mortgages. In our experience, all women fart under the sheets, cut their toe nails then leave the cuttings on the edge of the bath, prefer soap operas to football and object when you want to tour lap dancing clubs on a blokes night out.

'Just do it' is a great slogan for a global sports manufacturer with a swoosh as their motif but not the attitude to take when it comes to dumping your girlfriend, especially if there's hockey sticks or kitchen knives around.

If dumping her was something you thought up in a hot moment after a stupid argument you may wish to think things over again when you are cooler, or more realistically when you have sobered up.

> The thorny problem of girlfriend trouble is one that most of us men (unless hopelessly ugly or due to a lifestyle choice) encounter at one time or another.

Do you really want to dump her? How many of your CDs does she have? Get a piece of paper, fold it in two and make a list on each side, positives and negatives. On the plus side might be: You are getting good sex, she's easy on the eye, she pays your bills, she understands 4 4 2 and the sweeper system, she swallows. Surely under these circumstances, you can put up with smelly feet and the occasional snide remarks about your drinking habits? *(Eg."You're a sad lonely drunk, who's going to die alone, in a bedsit, in Hull!")*

There will of course be other items for the negative side of the paper. She may be two timing you. Or objecting to you two timing her. Or you may have met her family and been scared witless at the prospect of having to sit at a table with them over Xmas. She

may object to your eating pizza in bed. She may want too little sex, or too much. Put all this on the minus side of your list. Then weigh both sides up. How does it stack up? Still want to dump her? Great. You're reading the right book. You are prepared to put up with the life of a single bloke - the endless nights clubbing, the different girl every night from kinks to brunettes to blondes. Brilliant. You have looked into the future and its better without the current girl. She's got to be dumped. Sorted. The following chapters get down to the nitty gritty of ways and means. Follow this guide carefully. Your future happiness will depend on it.

CHAPTER 1

CHOOSING THE RIGHT DAY

Many men flounder when it comes to giving girls the heave. There are no college courses in dumping (although we wouldn't be surprised to see some in the future what with A-Levels getting easier and easier).

Your father never sat you on their lap and told you, 'this is how I dumped all the other women before I met your mum' (unless you have a weird dad). Most blokes blunder into a dump, with no thought of the day, or the time of day. Yet these things matter. They make a huge difference.

We will show you the options available to you. By seizing the initiative and choosing the day and time that are best suited for you, your split should bring far greater rewards.

Timings
* Birthdays
* Anniversaries
* Xmas
* New Year's Eve
* World Cup
* Valentines Day
* Exam times
* Early morning or late night
* Summer v Winter
* Her 'Time of the Month' factor

_____**Birthdays**

Her Birthday

Everyone wants their birthday to be memorable, but in reality so many birthdays turn out to be the same old same old, don't they? Dumping her on her birthday will make it a day she will never forget. Although she may be shocked at first, she will one day look back on the day as amazing. It will become something that she can laugh and tell her grandchildren about.

You however will become a dastardly figure in her family's folklore and live on from generation to generation as the bogey man of dating. Rest assured that by the time your story has been told and re-told and exaggeration has been piled on top of exaggeration you will not only have dumped her on her birthday but cut off one of her legs. But all that glory will come to you in the future, you need to concentrate on the matter in hand.

Plan the day with precision. If she's not having a party make sure you arrange one, for early evening. Such a party is sure to go on throughout the night so you can dump her late on in the party after you've had a great time partying. Dumping your girlfriend too early on her birthday is one of the mistakes novices make. What will happen in such a scenario is that she will get through all the crying in the morning, blow out the candles on her cake with tear-stained eyes in the afternoon while family and friends console her, and by evening she will be dancing like there's no tomorrow, celebrating her brand new start, with all her ex boyfriends ready to pounce on her again. She's having fun without you all too soon. Avoid this pain by dumping her at her party. If you get the timing exactly right you may even get some cake. And if you think dumping someone on their birthday is bad, spare a thought for Shakespeare who died on his.

Your Birthday
This is a perfect day. You have the ideal excuse: it's your birthday. People are meant to indulge themselves on their birthday. This could be the best present you ever give yourself.

But there is a problem with dumping a girlfriend on your birthday and that is knowing what to do with the present she no doubt has lovingly put a lot of time, effort and thought into getting you.

The Rule is: If it's an average present don't accept it, it's a tainted gift. Tell her to keep it, throw it away, smash it up, or whatever she feels like doing with it. That way you leave her with her head held high and dignity intact. Of course if it's something good like a holiday, then claim it as yours. You could take a friend in her absence, the sex might be different but you're likely to have a better time and because you're not heartless, remember to send her a postcard.

Anniversaries

Warranties run out after one year. We borrow credit on yearly deals. We change phone networks every twelve to eighteen months. So it makes sense to put your relationship on a similar clock. That way you can synchronise all the changes you need to make. Tidy beginnings and endings are so soothing in this world of chaos and unpredictability.

Ideally you will have mentioned at the beginning of the relationship that the relationship expiry date is exactly one year, with a two month cooling off period immediately prior to the break/renewal clause. It's always good to start a relationship as you mean to go on.

Not to worry if you didn't, just flag the date up four weeks beforehand (the same way the warranty companies send those reminder letters out) so that the dump day does not come right out of the blue for her.

One of the problems we men have is that we are crap with dates. Can't remember the date of your anniversary? Look in last year's diary if you kept it. If not, ask your girlfriend - women are very good at remembering anniversary dates. In fact women are very good at remembering EVERYTHING including what you said during a disagreement you had three years ago. '3 years 78 days 44 mins ago actually!'

Be careful how you ask her about the anniversary date. Play it as low key as possible. Otherwise she may get the impression you are planning a special treat to celebrate. She may even order a new dress ready for your surprise. Being dumped is probably not the surprise she has in mind. Actually, if your girlfriend is going to treat your question on anniversary dates as an indication of your commitment to the relationship, it is best not to ask at all.

Instead choose a date you feel is in the ball park and work from that. So long as she has not kept any factual evidence like tickets or receipts she will not be able to prove that the date you chose is not the correct anniversary date. You may have to tough this one out.

At the time of dumping her you might want to hand over a video or dvd of all your best moments together, as well as photos. A bit like when the contestants get booted out of the Big Brother House. If you can get Davina involved it might help her to come to terms with being dumped. Some girls really appreciate this kind of thing and you might get one last shag out of it. Others may not be so appreciative.

Xmas

The season of mince pies, tinsel and getting drunk with a religious excuse is a major time for break-ups, and with good reason. How much more entertaining than TV repeats and the Queen's Speech is the sight of couples having a good row, tearing each other to pieces then each storming out of the house swearing never to set eyes on each other ever again, even if it means having to live back at their Mum's caravan for a month.

Why is Xmas so popular for break-ups? There are many flashpoints. Being forced to share a strange meal with relatives you have chosen to avoid for eleven months with good reason is one. Having to play the happy Uncle and blow an amazing amount of money on presents for small nasty people called children that relatives drag with them, who are going to smash up their gifts as soon as you pull the door behind you is another. Having to kiss any grotty old girl who swings mistletoe your way is often the clincher.

Escaping from these nightmares would enable you to take up the many pleasures that Xmas has to offer a single guy. Parties, Parties and more Parties. Not forgetting all those tipsy party girls in party frocks and F*** Me thongs, looking for a handsome stranger (depending on what point in the night), to provide a little excitement over Xmas.

Xmas is a great time to be single. You can booze away for days on end without worrying you have to show your face at work. All you have to do is

> Dumping gets easier with practice

explain to your family you have just split up from your girlfriend and you need some 'me' time . Then you will be able to party AND duck the seasonal family squabble.

The best way to dump a girl at Xmas is in one short sharp burst. Say you can no longer hide the fact that you detest every member of her family and you feel rather than spoil a great day it is better that you two part. If she offers any counter arguments listen to them (nod and murmur 'I understand') then say you believe that family is destiny and that she will turn into her mum and since you detest her mum, you do not want to reach a point where you detest her so it is better you part now. Saying you detest her mum is the coup de grace for 95 percent of girls. They never go out with anyone who can't get on with their mum so that line guarantees you will be footloose and free over Xmas.

If the girl is in that rare 5% for whom the above reason does not work, invent a festive food related reason. For instance, say you've converted to militant veganism and will not sit at a table, let alone share a bed with a cannibal who is happy eating dead bird.

Explain away your love of KFC fried chicken as sins of the past. If she offers any counter arguments listen to her (nod and murmur 'I see I see') then quote her some of the vegan poet Benjamin Zephaniah's poetry featuring Turkeys Protesting Against Xmas.

Even if she doesn't believe you, she will accept that she is being dumped, rather than go out with someone who quotes poetry.

A Cautionary Note. From experience if you are going to use the 'I detest your mum' line, make sure she still has one, or you just come across as being sick.

Your one saving grace for dumping your girlfriend at Christmas is that at this time of year there are constant adverts for Careline, so you can party hard knowing at the very least she will have someone she can share her problems with.

New Year's Eve

New Year's Eve is a perfect time to dump your girlfriend. The phrase 'out with the old and in with the new' was made for such an occasion. Plus there are many parties on this night, with many single women looking to see the New Year in with a bang, as it were.

World Cup

There is no relationship worse than the one in which the woman hates the sport, such as football that you love. There is no worse time to discover this than on the cusp of the World Cup or European Championship Finals.

No girl is ever worth forsaking World Cup Finals for. It is a statement every football fan will agree with. Some alarmists say there is a girl shortage and only a fool would let a good girl go just because she doesn't appreciate the World Cup. Don't be fooled. There is no such 'girl shortage' out there, or at least we've never experienced this.

Yes, relationships are about compromise. But sacrificing the World Cup Finals is a compromise too far. Don't leave it until the Finals start. That's too late, especially if she owns the widescreen telly and takes it with her when she leaves you.

Test out her beliefs around this area as soon as possible, perhaps presenting it as a friendly, girly type questionnaire:

1)Ask her to reorganise your DVD shelf in order of most entertaining to least entertaining.

2)Tell her you want to share some family history. Say one of your distant Uncles died on the local football terraces, meat pie in mouth, waving a wooden rattle, watching a Division Two game.

3)During one of your long, dreamy chats one evening, ask her which she would prefer, a weekend in Paris or a week watching the World Cup Final in Bogota?

4)Finally try to sneak in the following questions during sofa time over lunch or while out shopping with her:

   When did England last win the World Cup?
   Who is Bobby Charlton?

Examine where she has placed your Greatest Football Games Ever Played DVDs. If they are at the awful end of the shelf, she has to go: she hates football. If she thinks the death of your fictitious Uncle sad rather than glorious, prefers Paris over Bogota and hasn't a clue about Bobby Charlton or 1966 then you have no hope for a successful relationship and you will need to kick this girl out of play speedily. Fill the house with football memorabilia, tape every match and refuse to watch anything other than the tapes or the Sky Sports channels and you will soon find her packing her bags.

PS. If you are Scottish, the bit about the World Cup probably doesn't apply to you.

Valentine's Day

Valentines Day is the biggest day in the romance calendar, loved by restaurateurs, rose sellers, card shops, gondola polemen, phone networks, cheesy rhymers, cocktail bars, light dimmer manufacturers, mattress makers, condom vendors, and linen sheet washers among others. But since when have you been a slave to tradition? Remember you are a maverick. Ditch your girlfriend the day before Valentine's Day and get working your address book to see which girls are available. Think back to the

many girls you fancied but only flirted, exchanged numbers with and only had phone sex with, because you never wanted to cheat on your girl. This is your time to take advantage.

After dumping your girlfriend ask her if she has booked a table for two at the French restaurant she mentioned she was planning to. If so, appeal to her reasonable side and persuade her to let you have it for you and your new girl. Explain tables at any half decent restaurant are hard to get on Valentine's Day and there's no real point in wasting a reservation.

Exam Times

For many hundreds of years monks, nuns and Islamic scholars were society's keepers of knowledge and with good reason: they never entered into heterosexual relationships and therefore knew nobody was going to start chucking ink pots at them and screw up their precious notes in a rage all because they had forgotten to buy fresh milk again.

So take your lead from them. If you have exams coming up and your relationship is stuttering, it is better to call time on it sooner rather than later. You will not be able to concentrate on revising while your blood pressure is raised by the prospect of her bursting through the door and picking another argument about something completely trivial like whose is the girl's underwear she has found under your bed. Apparently *"she has never possessed a purple thong"?* So I suppose you have learnt something new after all.

_____**Early morning or late night**

Morning

Fresh, clear thinking is always best achieved in the morning. Untangle yourself from your girlfriend, roll out of bed, build your strength up with a hearty breakfast, then wait for her to get up (unless you're in a rush for work), and tell her the news.

Without make up, or with smudged make up, she will look much uglier than usual, so serving her a personal eviction notice will be easier. Morning has the advantage of being the least sensual of hours. You will not be tempted to postpone the announcement for one more night of torrid sex, and you will not fall into the 'better sleep on it' reflex that comes over people in the evenings.

Morning is also the most practical time too. There is ample time for her to pack and move her stuff out onto the doorstep, and taxis are available at the normal rate.

If she cries, her cries will be less traumatic than at night and she may well find consolation while she is waiting for her taxi from one of the many 'heart and soul' TV shows like Trisha and Oprah. She will be able to arrange support and 'shoulder to cry' on services from her friends over lunch and she will still have three to four hours left for her favourite form of therapy, shopping. All things considered, morning is the smart time of day to dump her.

Late Night.

The best flight deals happen in the middle of the night, which might be worth remembering if you decide to dump your girlfriend at night and need to flee the country.

Even if you do not need to flee, night has its advantages. If the dump decision has been on your mind for a while, you will sleep much better once you have dumped her.

It is amazing how roomy and comfortable a double bed feels once you have got the freedom to roam all over it. Plus there's no arguments as to who sleeps in the wet patch.

If your girlfriend has any consideration she will keep the crying and shouting down to a minimum as it's night time. If not, remind her that the neighbours have a tiny baby who is sleeping and very sensitive to noise. Even if your neighbours don't have a baby say it anyway, she won't know for sure, no one knows their neighbours these days.

Late night works in terms of warding off your girlfriend's mother, close friends and other witches who may come round to berate you for dumping her. Being late at night it will appear believable when you fail to answer the banging on the door. Just pretend you are asleep or even better pretend they are Jehovah Witnesses and avoid at all costs.

PS: If you live in a half decent city, you can dump her and go clubbing right afterwards.

_____**Summer v Winter**

Summer

Summer comes along gloriously hot and there are girls, girls, girls everywhere, in the skimpiest of outfits. The Result: Not cheating is infinitely harder in Summer than Winter. Our survey has found that if you are going to succumb to the charms of another girl, for some reason it's more likely to happen when there is more naked flesh on display. If you are constantly going to be tempted by these Sunshine Sheilas it is better to clear the decks, girlfriend wise, first, ready to take on board the new season's fresh talent.

Why does this happen? It could be that you have never really had a good look at your girlfriend in the flesh in all the time you have known her. If you met in Autumn and have been getting jiggy with each other with the lights out, and if she has been getting up much earlier than you, and if you have not been sharing showers, then you may only know your girlfriend by feel. (Actually our surveys show women love a guy who has got sensitive, feeling hands, which we hasten to add is not the same as liking a groper).

If this is the case it will come as either a surprise or a shock when she eventually strips off for the Summer. If it's a surprise, lucky you, your 'fit girl underneath loads of clothes' instincts paid off. If it's a shock, wise up. Dump her quickly. You can celebrate Summer with a new girl to go to Glastonbury / Reggae Sunsplash / PimpHo Tour and all the open air dance festivals with.

PS. You will need to move quickly as our Summers are generally short and crap!

Winter

Trees shed leaves in Winter. Snakes shed skins. Tired things die off. This is Nature's Law. If your relationship has been unsatisfactory through Summer and struggled into Autumn, Winter will kill it off. You will be cooped up in each other's company far more often when it gets icy cold outside. All those flashpoints you have managed to avoid by skipping out to visit friends will loom larger and larger. You are both biting your tongue, trying not to ignite the big row, but as sure as eggs is eggs, it's going to kick off. You may as well quicken the process.

By dumping her you will be doing both of you a favour, putting an end to the niggly rows and replacing them perhaps with one big, air clearing, relationship splitting, almighty row.

Girls often feel miserable and upset when you dump them. This is all the more reason to do the dump in Winter. Winter was made for feeling blue. It is a season of discontent and dissatisfaction. If your girlfriend is a blues singer it is your duty to dump her in Winter rather than Summer. The more intensely she experiences the split up the more charged her singing will become. You might even get a mention in the album sleeve.

If she doesn't speak to you for weeks after, walks the other way when she sees you on the street, this too is natural. Winter is a time of withdrawal, of hibernation. She will emerge, renewed and invigorated in Spring. But thankfully you will be free of her.

Other seasons: a girl for every season.
It is the call of all young men to play the field. They date as many girls as possible, hoping to discover a girl who clicks in all the right places, and licks in all the right places. Without this exploration they may get trapped in a long term relationship with the wrong girl and end up married, mortgaged and miserable.

It is this pursuit of happiness that drives men to date as many girls as possible early on in life. What better way of bringing some structure to this chaos than by dating one girl per season?

Miss Spring might love walking in sudden showers, watching Wimbledon, all things Valentine and be brilliant at scoffing Easter eggs. Miss Summer might have a hotline to the best raves the best open air concert tickets, might love stripping off to bare essentials as soon as there is a glint of sun, might like super cold showers, outdoor sex and barbecue parties. Miss Autumn could love to dress in black, chant Halloween spells, be really into football league positions, and love storms and floods. Miss Winter could be big and fat to keep you warm in bed, enjoy snowball fighting, super hot showers and getting up early in the morning to heat your clothes up in the dryer before you put them on. Which goes to show there really is a girl for every season out there. It's just rarely the same girl.

Her 'Time of the Month' factor

Try to steer clear of dumping her during her PMT. This may be harder than you think as some girlfriends seem to be constantly on their periods. Never just come out and ask, as this appears to annoy them, whether they are or aren't. Our advice is to keep a log of the number of tampons in the house at any one time. A decrease in numbers and bingo.

The problem with dumping her when she's on is that her emotions will be more intense at this time. In addition to this she may feel bloated and ugly and start blaming these factors for the split instead of the actual reasons like her constant nagging, lack of personality, clinginess etc....

CHAPTER 2

PLANNING

Planning is everything here. Dumping your girlfriend can be a confusing time. Your body will be confused anticipating her not pressing up to you at night any longer. Your wallet will be confused at the thought she will no longer be paying all your bills. And your fridge will be confused knowing soon there will be no more green things in it.

Amid all this confusion, you can make serious logistical errors unless you are prepared. You need to plan both how you will get your stuff out of the apartment (or her stuff if she's the one moving out); and where you (or she) will be staying once she is dumped. Details are everything. If you are the one doing the leaving, your plans will need to take in whether you will leave suddenly (the big bang method), or slowly (the slow disappearance technique). In full, this chapter will cover:

* The Big Bang method of leaving
* Slow Disappearance Techniques
* Forward Addressing
* Friends, Pets & Children
* Never Keep Notes
* The Importance of Black Bags

Big Bang

This method has the glory of simplicity. If you move out all in one go, it cuts down on the aggravation that occurs from a more drawn out departure. The latter often involves having to constantly console her, having to argue and debate the rights and wrongs of your move, and having to hunt behind the back of the sofa for possessions of yours she has hidden out of sheer petty vindictiveness.

The moonlight dump has its attractions. If she loves to party until 3am, bide your time and, as soon as she has left the house in her party dress and her *'don't even think of suggesting I should stop in with you and watch your miserable football game'* scowl, get on the phone to a taxi firm. Order the biggest eight seater they have got.

Then phone the most trustworthy mates you have and explain your situation. If you have a mate who has been in the army so much the better because army guys know how to move fast and shift stuff at a moment's notice. They also tend to be good drinkers, but that's another matter. Don't use any friends who are working for chat lines, social services or any of the counselling industries: they will want you to talk it over and you'll still be talking when she gets back legless and all loved up from her clubbing. She might look drop dead sexy in this situation and you could slip into 'let's postpone this till morning' mode.

An alternative would be to check her diary. If she is going to be away for two weeks in Ayia Napa or hospital move out in that period. You will be under less pressure and will be able to pack at your own pace.

Slow Disappearance

This requires more guile. You will be doing smuggler-like runs in and out of the house in an over-large coat hiding your CD rack, potted plants and favourite kitchen gadgets.

With luck she may not notice the slow disappearance of your stuff from the shared apartment. So long as you don't remove or adjust any photos of the two of you together you should be ok. Women are remarkably sensitive about photos.[1] They notice instantly if they have been moved or even looked at in a sceptical manner.

If she cottons on that your stuff is slowly disappearing, there are various ruses you might be able to employ to throw her off the scent: the Oxfam Ruse, the Decluttering Lie, the Ebay Story and the Trainee Monk Explanation.

The Oxfam Ruse

This goes, *'I've started working as an Oxfam volunteer and they're running low on donations. My growing sense of world morality has moved me to fill some black bags for them.'* Don't go overboard on this, else she may start donating her own stuff too, and then blame you for her being clotheless on top of everything else when you dump her. For authenticity buy in Fair Trade tea, or do what Coldplay's Chris Martin does and write messages on your hands. Maybe a subtle message like 'Time for Change'.

The Decluttering Lie

Tell your soon-to-be ex that *'I've been watching one of those How To Live Your Life Better TV shows fronted by [any C List celebrity, probably Claire Sweeney] and realise the root cause of my unhappiness, lack of job, inability to relate to people properly and general insignificance in the grand scheme of things is that I have not decluttered my life'*. For authenticity tell her declutter is the new detox.

---

[1] Especially photos you 'accidentally' send to all your friends in your phone book

The eBay Story

Say you have discovered the joy of ebay. People are putting in ridiculously high offers for your stuff, and you are making a mint selling it all off. For one-upmanship, claim the highest bids are coming for the items she's always hated. This ploy carries risks. She may ask you to show her the money you've made and she will probably expect you to spend it on her. To get round this, say you are planning a romantic holiday away together, no expenses spared. Dump her two days before this fictitious holiday date. It may infuriate her but as we all know it's a cruel world out there and who better than you, her new ex, to point this out.

Trainee Monks Vow of Poverty

A common entry requirement of Orders of Monks is that you sell off all your worldly goods since you will be living in the spiritual not the material world. Say you are doing weekends at the monastery first of all to see if it is for you and so are testing how it feels to own less stuff at the same time. Don't get too specific. Some Orders of Monks also have vows of chastity and she may declare her support for your spiritual journey by withdrawing all sexual contact. If lately you have not been getting any (with her), then that may not be a big deal. Otherwise pedal softly on this one: we assume you want to keep getting your end away with her right up to the final dumping.

Forward addressing: You

If you are the one moving out, then making sure you will have a place to stay is crucial. You may need to start widening your circle of friends. Ideally you will discover a mate with a mansion who's looking for a drinking buddy. If not, you'll have to start reacquainting with the ones you had before the girlfriend informed you they weren't suitable. Begin by inviting yourself round all your friend's houses, checking them out for spare rooms, fridge size, and any fatal quirks like keeping lizards in the bath or, worse, over-cleanliness. If you have any half fanciable single women

within your circle of friends see if you can get a foot in there. Maybe you will be able to move in with her as 'just friends' and then watch the relationship blossom from there. This is the plot of many Hollywood films so there must be truth in it (though having said that, we've yet to meet a prostitute like Julia Roberts in Pretty Woman, despite extensive research).

If you're extremely lucky you'll get free lodging, free sex and a cooked breakfast every day. It's a rare woman who will put out that much in this mean spirited age and you may quickly be accused of being a slobby, selfish, sex mad leech. If this happens, buy your host some perfume off a market stall and she'll soon come round.

If friends fail you, the next option is hotels. They do good deals for long stayers, though in the long run they work out expensive. On the other hand, cleaning is thrown in and there's room service all hours, decent vending machines in the lobby and you don't have to faff about choosing curtains and stuff.

The last resort is of course your mum. She may do a lot of sighing and *'when am I going to get you off my hands and where's my grandchildren?'* But tough it out, in her heart she likes you living in your old bedroom even if she was thinking of converting into a pottery studio. Tell her that, with her arthritis, the chances of her making any decent vases would be minimal, then smile winningly. She'll come round. She's your mum. If not, buy her some perfume.

Forward addressing: Her

Find out her mum's address then get some labels printed with your soon-to-be ex's name combined with her mum's address. When dumping her show her the labels. This will calm her fears about her post going astray. The Post Office also do a marvellous and highly reliable Redirection Service at a very low price. Just in case her mum's place proves unavailable get a list of youth hostels and student tourist hotels. Also, get hold of the local Storage Centre phone number. All this paperwork should be ready to hand to her with the labels when you give her the heave.

> Logistics is the science
> of preparation

Regarding her stuff, if her mum lives in a very small house and there is no room for it all, do not agree to keep her stuff at yours 'until she sorts something out'. This will only mean she'll be traipsing through your life picking stuff up for months on end. Instead, drive her stuff to a storage depot and pay for the first three months storage. (It's usually half price for the first three months). She'll appreciate the gesture and this is not a time to be cheap: you will be saving yourself endless petty aggravation.

Friends, Pets & Children

If you've been in a relationship for a while you may have mutual friends. If this is the case you will need to secure your friends pre-dump. The general rule with friends, a bit like with money in divorces, you keep the friends you had before the relationship, as does she, but the friends made during your time as boyfriend/girlfriend are up for grabs. You'll need to get the ones you like onside before she does.

Pets are similar to money in court cases in that many a relationship split has resulted in a court battle with people fighting for custody of 'Tyson' or whatever people call their pets. The way the judge often decides in such cases is to get the couple to shout the pet's name and see which one it goes to. What you need to do is, weeks leading up to the dump, keep calling your pet and giving it a treat every time it comes to you. Thus ensuring that in court it will come to you.   PS. We don't think this works with fish.

With children it is different, let her have them.

Never Keep Notes

Never keep notes of your dumping plans (or ones to rob a bank). Women think nothing of reading your diary, rooting through your trouser pockets and going through your emails and Word files. They will say it is because they simply want to understand you better. It's actually because they are very nosey.

Nothing gives the game away more than a list found in your Levi's that reads:

To Do:
Get all my CDs safe
Empty joint account
Book space for her stuff at Safestore
Change locks
Tell her she's dumped

If you are this indiscreet you need a lot of help: why not buy another copy of this book.

If your girl is excessively into reading your diary, emails and stuff, use her curiosity to your advantage. Throw her off the scent by writing short paeans of praise to her in your work diary. Create a fictitious email friend called Steve and send him emails that sigh with desire for your girl and say you want to spend till eternity with her. Add that it is only your natural shyness that holds you back from saying these things to her face. Your girl will bask in her new, 'secret knowledge' that you are besotted with her. Meanwhile you can carry on smuggling out the CD's etc you bought jointly that are otherwise going to be the subject of loud disputes when you dump her.

If you absolutely have to keep To Do lists, keep them

electronically and password-protect them. Do not use the same password for this To Do file as the one you use for your cash card. She probably knows that one already. She will also know all your banking passwords such as Date of Birth, Mother's Maiden Name and Favourite Food since you will have said them loads of times when in a drunken state ordering pizza over the phone and she will have heard them all. (This doesn't work in reverse as you will barely know her birthday, never mind her mum's maiden name). Instead invent a completely fresh password. A final word of advice on this: **do not** keep this in a file marked 'secret passwords'.

The Importance Of Black Bags

One of you will soon be moving out. This cannot physically happen unless the right containers are available for making that move. Black bags vary in quality and size. But generally, ten black bags is enough to stuff your clothes in. If it's her stuff, then make that forty.

If you are expecting her to be moving out, have a fat roll of cheap bin liners ready so that when she bursts into a flood of tears complaining, *'but how can I move all this stuff?'* you can pull them out and say, 'hey presto, problem solved'. She'll really appreciate that.

Cheer her up by pointing out prisoners leave prison carrying their stuff out of the prison gates in bin liners for a reason: the bags double up as excellent temporary shelters and sleeping bags, useful knowledge for those without forward accommodation.

If she's not got a car, we've always found shopping trolleys are a good substitute for transporting the aforementioned black bags. You can get them from supermarkets for a pound or, if she's a cheapskate, they can usually be found on train tracks or in the local canal.

CHAPTER 3

WHAT KIND OF GIRL ARE YOU DUMPING?

There are as many varieties of girl as there are varieties of flowers or pizza boxes. Each flower has its own scent and attractiveness, each pizza box has a different way of opening. When you come to pick a flower it pays to know where to hold the stem, whether the stem has barbs or little nettle like thorns on it. With pizza boxes some observation of the different flaps and folds will save you fumbling around for ages and getting a great mess on your lap.

Similarly with girls there's no point trying some one size fits all formula for dealing with dumping girls. Girls will deal with it differently, depending on what type of girl they are. These are the types we have identified:

* Screamers
* Bawlers
* Bunny boilers
* Fatalists
* Shruggers
* Deniers
* Couch psychologists

Screamers

If she screams when you forget her birthday, screams when you 'forget' to pick her up from the shopping centre and screams when you 'accidentally' spend the holiday money on tinted windows for your car, you can bet she's going to scream when you tell her she's dumped. The smartest advice is simple. Don't fight the screaming. Instead choose an environment where her screaming will fit in.

Here are two case studies:

Dave took his girlfriend into the countryside on a windy Autumn night, on the pretence of going camping. They pitched their tent on a hill where the winds were already howling and there was no-one but sheep for an audience. Dave told her she was dumped there. Her screams were indistinguishable from the wind and heard only by sheep (and Dave).

Andy took his girlfriend to a horror movie at the multiplex on a Saturday afternoon when it was packed with jumpy teenage girls and told her about sixty five minutes into the film (when all the seriously big scream scenes start kicking in). Everyone thought it was the film and not Andy's message that got her goat. The cinema audience all loved her and egged her on.

Try to leave her when she's got tonsilitis. Even screamers will think twice about howling when their tonsils are oozing with pus and the smallest intake of breath feels like being kicked by a brick-shoed camel.

Practical Tip
Wax earplugs are far more effective than the sponge ones at blocking out screams. Ask the chemist if they stock plugs that block high frequency.

_____**Bawlers**

Whereas the basic message of screamers is, 'I'm going to kill you for this', and embarrass you into the bargain, bawlers are more into the pity side of things.

They are saying, 'here I am, a put upon, beaten down little girl, who even Bob Geldolf can't rescue. A girl whose world has come crashing down, all because of this cruel ogre (That's you).'

Your natural human instinct that comes from the innate kindness all men have, is to put your arm around her and say, *'give us a smile, you'll get over it, you'll meet someone else'* etc. The danger of this manoeuvre is you may continue giving sympathy up to the point where you find yourself agreeing to not leave her, and everything is back on. The girl has used tears to successfully 'undump' herself. You have been tactically outmanoeuvred.

This outcome is regrettable and avoidable if you use the proper

Daniel-Pumpkin tactics for bawlers. Firstly, try to make sure your girlfriend has a girl friend present when you dump her (a girl friend rather than a male friend as the male friend might punch you when you tell her she's dumped and she bursts into tears).

A girl friend will be able to supply all the sympathy, cuddles and *'he's a bastard didn't I tell you, you're well rid of him'* needs of the bawling ex girlfriend, leaving you to exit the scene in a speedy and dignified manner. This scenario is made all the more neat and tidy if the girl that you are dumping the ex for happens to be the same girl supplying the ex's sympathy needs. This way the new girlfriend can head off the ex's revenge ideas with a timely *'he's not worth it, don't lower yourself to his level'* or at least forewarn you if the heading off tactics do not work.

If the newly ex'd is bawling her pretty eyes out and her relatives come round mid-bawl, drop Robbie Williams' Angels on the CD player and say she's just realised the beauty of the voice and the enormity of the lyrics, then leave sharpish. Try not to let your finger slip and play 'Let Me Entertain You' instead.

Bunny Boilers

There are six levels of revenge your dumped girlfriend might aspire to, each level worse than the one before. If you are lucky it stops at stage one. But heeding the old adage it's better to be safe than sorry we will examine all five stages and give some tips on how to deal with them.

Level 1: Divine retribution. This is the mildest form of revenge and is where the ex wills fervently for divine retribution to strike you down dead, but leaves the actual delivery of the punishment to

God. (Like God hasn't got anything better to do).

Along similar lines is your ex buying a voodoo doll and sticking pins in the doll and imagining your writhing with each puncture of the pin. The bunny boiler stage 1 might also go to an astrologer seeking evil predictions about you. All these are the workings of a superstitious but harmless mind.

Faced with this, it does no harm to spread a rumour that you have had various misfortunes befall you (eg broke a leg, lost your wallet, pranged your car) since the split up. To add realism make sporadic movements. At the very least you will gain yourself some space on public transport. The superstitious ex can feel her voodoo has worked and will therefore achieve smug satisfaction, also known as 'closure' and move on.

Level 2: the scandal-monger. This is a stage stronger in the bunny boiler stakes. It is the girl who, post break-up, can't help but spread juicy tit bits about your sexual performance to all her friends at parties. You may detect this is happening if girls giggle while looking or pointing to your crotch then spin away from you in guffaws. Chances are your ex has spread stories that your dick is non-performing.

Solution: Whip it out there and then and prove your manhood is up to the job. [JD] Or more wisely perhaps, confess it is all true and that you seek a considerate female lover who can handle at least sixty minutes foreplay while you get your apparatus fully hard: you should see the girls all flocking back to your side. [HP]

> **Warning**
> Following one of the above two pieces of advice may lead to a court appearance.

Level 3: scissors and paint girl. If your girlfriend likes DIY and always has paint and a pair of those giant wallpaper scissors handy, then there is a fair chance she will employ these tools to express her displeasure at the break up.

So at least one month before the date of dump, replace your wardrobe of designer labels with old clothes from Oxfam. Then dump her. This way if she seeks revenge with scissors she'll home in on the charity shop stuff and it's no loss to you. Do however get your designer stuff back from your Mum's once the ex's scissors frenzy is over. You don't want to see your dad walking around town in your suits.

Some women are more into paint than wallpaper. It is harder to guard against the paint thrower since they have so many more potential targets. Immediately after dumping, change the locks on your front door. Store your car in a garage for a week.
If you stop at a junction and see her with a tin of paint, waving at you, don't think she's about to ask you whether Pink Sunset will look better than Burnt Sienna on her dining room walls. DRIVE OFF FAST!

> **DIY Alert**
> If your girlfriend likes DIY there may be other, more fundamental reasons why things aren't working out between the two of you.

Level 4: bank account girl. This is a 'finger on buzzers' situation. Whoever gets to the joint bank account first will win. As the Dumper, not the dumpee, you have the advantage of surprise on your side. Casually farm in all plastic debit cards you may be sharing with her, then either (a) clear all money out of the accounts or (b) change all the password numbers to prevent her accessing them.

Option A is safer than option B, because if she does one of her crying routines down the phone the bank people might not be able to resist her and will unblock the account for her and block you instead. We speak from very very bitter personal experience.

Level 5: web shaming girl. This form of revenge combines the public humiliation element of the old English stocks (where people were dragged to the village square, locked between two blocks of wood and pelted with fruit) with the technological power of the web.

Ex girlfriends are able to use the Internet to tell the world at great length their extremely one sided version of the relationship, a version which is always spiced with bias, exaggerations and whopping great lies. She might visit Friends ReUnited and write something up about you or create her own website and upload letters you wrote and photos of you in an uncompromising light, recounting everything negative that happened, how evil you are and how low she is feeling.

Solution: Take the moral high ground. To anybody who reads her web ramblings or views compromising photos say, 'very little that you read on the web is true, and photos are always being retouched'. If this fails, set up your own website. That way at least people will get both sides of the story. OK, you both end up looking ridiculous and it may turn into a soap opera, but that's no bad thing, as a nation we love soaps. Even Hollyoaks gets viewers.

Level 6: axe chucker-bunny boiler girl. There is little that will deflect this girl from exacting revenge on you. A few things might delay her. At least a month before the dump, implant in her mind the idea that revenge is a dish best served extremely cold. Repeat this thinking until she comes to agree with it. It's the power of repetition - much used by advertisers and young children.

Then hope that by the time you dump her the idea has sunk in and she waits before acting against you. This strategy buys you time. You can move town, city or country in the gap.

Make sure when you dump her there is some physical distance between you eg dump by phone or by text. If that is not possible, have the dump conversation while standing outside a police station, or at least the emergency ward of a major hospital.

Safer still, try to get her to dump you. That way she'll feel no need for revenge.

If all these things fail, most Army and Navy stores now do a range of anti-knife vests that are remarkably unobtrusive and often lined with Goretex for added comfort. Most axe-chucking takes place within the first six months of a dump, so it is generally safe to take the vest off after this.

In the meantime, to any potential suitors, make out you are a small time gangster (women love a bad man), or recently recruited into MI6 (women love a man of mystery) or working Undercover for a television company (women love a man on TV), and that's why you have to wear the vest. Do not under any circumstances say you are scared of the ex, because some people might snigger and call you a cissy. If this ever happens to you, don't panic: find a responsible adult like your mummy and tell them.

Fatalists

The reaction of this group can be unnerving. They foresaw you were going to dump them. Their star sign had been warning about it for ages.

Turn their belief in fate to your advantage. They may see you dumping them as a punishment from God. They may call your ending of the relationship a result of karma: a slap in the face for them from the Spiritual Power for bad things they have done earlier in life. If you want to relieve them of this sense of guilt, you could say the split up is not about them, it's about you. But what good is this going to do you? The better option is to keep your mouth shut and allow them to continue to blame themselves.

Some useful and assuaging words in this scenario are: *'yes, I agree with you, there is a Higher Force than either of us controlling these things'*. One other fairly effective line is, *'we can neither predict nor fathom the wisdom of the Divine Mind/the Gaiea/the One'*.

Then leave quickly before your shallow understanding of her belief system is exposed and her anger multiplies so much she becomes an axe chucking bunny boiler (see above).

Shruggers

Some women take being dumped in their stride. They will shrug, perhaps help you pack your things, then wave you off with a friendly smile. It is rare to discover a partner like this, but they do exist. They are simply gifted with a greater than average understanding of the situation, or stoned. They find no great need for melodrama or histrionics. They accept your word and decision as wise and move on to practical matters.

It is not that they never held a candle for you. You still make their heart beat faster every time you enter a room. They may well be head over heels in love with you. But their huge respect for you means they will not make a scene or embarrass you in any way nor contemplate challenging your executive decision that the relationship is over.

PS. on shruggers: this lack of emotion, and desire to deal with the practical things, is the nearest many men get to partaking in a same sex relationship.

Deniers

The denier will ignore your announcement and continue planning the joint birthday parties, joint purchase of a one bedroom nest close to all amenities, continue pushing to meet your parents and want to know the birthdays of your little nieces and nephews so she can send cards on behalf of both of you.

You must use clear language with a girl who is a denier. Try, *'I am leaving you. We are finished'* followed by a long pause. If you get no response, check she does not have her IPod buried in her ears and that she is not watching the climax to her favourite 'Rom Com'. Then try again. Use the exact same words, and again pause to ensure the message sinks in. Then pack.

You may find yourself three days later, still at the joint apartment,

sharing a bath with her and removing her corns while thinking, *'did we actually have that conversation?'*
If so, it is because you failed to follow through. Deniers treat all statements as provisional, tentative expressions of fantasy rather than clear cold statements of actual intent.

Do not succumb to any postponement of the split. Do not allow one last visit to the cinema together, or a rendez vous at a café to discuss things again. These rendez vous usually morph into the same old smooching, holding of hands and carrying on as if the dump speech was never made. Some men have been trying to dump their girlfriends for years and fail so miserably, that ten years later they are still together AND they have three children in toe, all due to the denier's subtle and effective tactics.

Couch psychologists

This girl will beckon you to sit beside her on the couch or more often at the kitchen table, then she will take out a pen and notepad, and, with trembling lips and a thoughtful, innocently enquiring look, she will ask you to recount where you felt it all went wrong.

This girl has probably sat through hundreds of Trisha and Oprah shows. She will have heard the most fancy theories about why relationships break up and she will want to work her way carefully through her checklist. She will call your discussions 'sessions'. You will be expected to sign up for at least three. Be wary.

She will go through your childhood, your relationship with your mother and father, whether you get on with your siblings, how you felt about school, a list of your previous relationships and why in your view they failed. Before you know it she will diagnose commitment phobia as a result of: (a) your mother's neglect of you (b) from when your sister stabbed you with a fork in the sand pit at Butlins, (c) excessive co-masturbation with boyhood chums,

or (d) narcissism-vanity issues.

Allow all her psycho babble to wash over you. Repeat silently in your mind your mantra, 'It's over, me and you are finished.' Once she has exhausted her speculations, repeat your mantra aloud.

Do not turn this into a battle. Do not reply to her allegations of commitment issues by giving her detailed examples of her clingyness. She knows more psycho-babble than you and you will be hopelessly outgunned in any argument containing long words.

Don't feel guilty about it. You have supplied her with much raw material for her psychology essays, if nothing else. Whatever you do, DON'T agree to meet in a TV studio to 'discuss things further'. She will know better than you how to work the studio crowds and the audience will eat you alive.

CHAPTER 4

FACE TO FACE DUMPING

F ace to face dumping is the choice of the hero and the warrior. It is heroic because no matter how carefully you prepare your speech to her, you cannot predict how she will react. You will be vulnerable to thrown plates and IPods, beatings around the head, screams, taunts, and the firing of pistols. Even heroes take precautions.

The general advice here is to think carefully about location. For instance, dumping her while you are both swimming in the local municipal pool is good as there are few blunt instruments to hand. Similarly smart would be the municipal Peace Gardens while a troupe of Buddhists is present, or while you are both visiting someone in Intensive Care. This last option has a dual purpose, firstly she can't kick off in a hospital and secondly seeing someone desperately clinging to life, will give her some perspective: she will realise that there are worse things in the world than never having sex with you again.

This chapter considers some of the most popular and effective locations for face to face dumping.

* In bed, after sex
* In bed, before sex
* In the bath
* On a bus
* On campus
* In a canteen
* In a car

* In a club
* At your wedding
* At Someone Else's Wedding
* In church
* On Holiday
* At A Funeral

In bed after sex

This is have your cake and eat it territory and is fully recommended. If you have not lined up another girl to take the place of the one you are dumping then you cannot be certain you are going to have sex any time soon except with yourself. Therefore it is only wise to drink your last long fill at the fountain of sex before venturing out into a potential famine.

An added benefit of this approach is that good sex often makes women languid and drowsy.[2] So much so that after having sex, women pay little attention to what you are saying. (This may continue way after sex). Instead they tune into the tone in which you are speaking. Understanding this allows you to dump them gently, indeed so gently they may barely notice it. Murmur your speech while stroking her gently and she will probably turn over, curl up and say, 'yes, whatever, go ahead'.

There is the possibility (never encountered by the authors we hasten to add) that you may not have fully satisfied your girl in bed. In which case she is likely to be a little grouchy and

[2]If you are not sure how to provide good sex, wait for our next book, 'How To Drive Your Women Wild In Bed'

frustrated and quick tempered. Under such circumstances she will take being dumped as a blessing.

She might even say that she's glad because now she can move on to a boyfriend who can last longer than two minutes. Don't be too down hearted, you've had what the professionals call a 'Result', you've dumped her AND had sex. And as long as you've been satisfied sexually what else really matters?

In bed before sex

This is a much trickier proposition. Being dumped is not a natural aphrodisiac. It will not make her feel sexy and up for sex.

Do not say anything facetious like *'let's do it once more for old time's sake'* or *'let me feel the goods one last time'* or even worse, *'let me slip it in so you remember what you're going to be missing'*. This is too similar to Jim Bowen's catchphrase in Bullseye "Here's what you would have won" to be effective. Take it from us no woman wants to be thinking about Jim Bowen when they're in bed.

> The best warriors prepare thoroughly

You need to employ the subtle, skills of a silver tongued Casanova, to pull this one off. It is not going to be easy but remember God loves a tryer.

Try arguing that your incompatibility is lifestyle and not sex so why throw out the baby with the bath water? For example she might be a fox hunting Tory while you are a Ban the Bomb Leftie, or she's loaded and constantly dripping in bling while you live hand to mouth. Or she mixes with grungy riff raff, while for you no party is complete without champagne, ballroom gowns and bow ties.

None of these should be an automatic bar on continuing the sex. Try pitching to her that: *'we have the same sexual appetites and quirks so we both have a lot to lose by splitting completely. The chances of us finding another partner who likes morning sex with leather spanking and cucumbers is remote.* So let's split but hang onto the sex bit for both our sakes. What do you say?'

If she says yes, well done, you lucky boy, get your tackle out and get down to business. If she says, no, don't lose hope, be prepared for a drunken late night call one day soon.

> Thinking of Jim Bowen in bed is one way men can avoid premature ejaculation

In the bath

Bubble baths are one of the most magnificent relaxing inventions man has ever come up with. Sharing a bath creates intimacy and honesty. For example, if you are in a bath with your girlfriend and you say you're ending the relationship because you no longer fancy her, there's no point sitting there with a huge erection. It confuses things.

The advantage of dumping in a bath is that it is very hard to hurt someone while swishing bubbles and sloshing water. Nevertheless, be careful when she says she's searching for the soap under the water, because it won't be the suds that brings tears to your eyes.

Many women believe in the power of aromatherapy. So why don't you run your girlfriend a nice bath. Chuck in the entire bottle of ylan ylang crystals, passion flower crème, evening primrose bubbles or whatever fad she currently favours. The more relaxed she is the better.

Tell her to get in, whilst you disappear. Once you are sure she's nice and relaxed, return to the bathroom fully clothed and break your news, then leave the flat. Before leaving you could add cold water to the bath, in a symbolic representation that things have cooled between the two of you. She may think you are just being a bastard. Again.

On a bus

Buses are great for interruptions, they provide 'gazing mournfully out of a window' moments, and have a natural stop-start rhythm that can help you with your dumping speech. Like a bus, you may get held up, but like a bus you get started again and if you act confidently and in the advised manner you will find dumping her as easy as cruising in a bus lane.

First choose the stop you want to get off at. Work backwards from that. Early morning buses are ideal. Most people riding these are depressed at having to do another day's work. These work zombies are unlikely to react if your speech sets off a bout of screaming from your newly ex girlfriend. They will merely believe they are imagining it, that it is all in their head, their mood music to the sight of the approaching call centre gates.

Late night buses are a different kettle of fish and are to be avoided wherever possible (whether you are dumping someone or not). Debates, discussions, duels and fights break out between 'high spirited' strangers here. If you dump her on the 'red eye' bus, do not be surprised if you find yourself in a kangaroo court once your girlfriend tells all and sundry you are dumping her. At the very least, try to stay on the lower deck. Ring the bell immediately you have told her and pray the bus stops before the lynch mob gets going.

On campus

Students split up all the time. And they are among the most intelligent people in society. One of the unique aspects of University is the sheer range and numbers of students attending.

A final year statistics student[3] told us that the chance of finding your ideal partner with your first relationship are so low as to be negligible. And the chances of two ill matched people being unhappy together is so high it is off the scale. Therefore, the greatest happiness to the greatest number is best brought about by individuals sleeping around as frequently as possible. QED.

The best location to dump your student belle is the Student Union bar. All parties involved in the Dump can drown their sorrows with cheap lager while running their eye over possible new girl/boyfriends. .

Another aspect of campus life is that they provide an atmosphere of tolerance and understanding. You will also find they provide a high percentage of fit, single women up for a bit of fun now you've moved on from the ex.

In a canteen

Canteens generally stock food you have to endure and hack through. Stench producing boiled greens, globby steamed fish, congealed baked beans and cement hard pizza are just some canteen staples.

Canteens do not encourage dreamers, romantics or wishful thinkers. There are no roses or violinists. Instead there are buzzing fluorescent lights, clattering cutlery, trundling trolleys and scraping chairs. A canteen is a place to be pragmatic, down to earth, matter of fact. They are noisy places, full of guffaws and yelling, pranksters and office show-offs trying out their latest wacky trick.

[3]The statistics student in question went on to pass his exams, gaining a very high Third, so we can safely say he knew what he was talking about.

Amidst this din and bedlam, your girlfriend shouting at you when you tell her she is dumped will hardly be noticed. Any tears will be put down to the toxicity of the egg fried rice rather than emotional trauma. Canteens also have many fire exits: useful if you sense danger and need  to leave quickly. Contrast canteens with libraries. Never use a library for dumping a girl. All the nerds will hear and tut tut and there is only one exit.

In a car

Think carefully if you are considering dumping her while she is at the wheel. We know women find driving a tricky enough prospect at the best of times, without having to deal with being dumped as well. You wouldn't want to be responsible for her mowing down an unsuspecting pedestrian and so losing her no claims bonus.

Instead make sure you are at the wheel yourself. Preferably parked up at a quiet lay-by, within walking distance of a bus stop so she can get home once you have dumped her. If the car is in motion ensure you are on a quiet country road. Be particularly careful about the music you choose. It should be calm, positive upbeat stuff, not the latest doom filled ditty from Radiohead. If you have air conditioning whack it on full: it will cool down what may be a hot moment.

Being mobile when you dump a girl has many advantages. For a start you can pretend you are a tour guide. You can tailor your route accordingly. For example, you could drive past the pub you first met, or the Drive Thru you treated her to on your first date, or the cemetery where you first did it AND got her some flowers. At the end of the nostalgia trip you could say, *"This relationship has now terminated"*. If you can say this in a number of foreign languages it will add to the tour guide feel.

Please Note: if you ever get your girlfriend flowers from the cemetery, don't go for a wreath that reads out NANA: she will smell a rat.

In a club

Dance music and dumping were made for each other. In the frenzy of the beat, as heavenly, multi-scented bodies press and rub and jiggle and flaunt to the roar of a classic Summer hit, bellowing out over the music 'I AM LEAVING YOU!', will have zero effect on her. If she is the rhythm queen you know her to be, she will simply nod and go on dancing, maybe turning away from you and enticing other boys to come synchronise moves with her. Clubs more than anywhere else illustrate the fact there are plenty of takers for a sexy, fun girl and your parting from her is no big loss once she gets used to the idea, which in clubs can be in seconds.

You may even find yourself jealous of the other lads who start moving in. Resist this unworthy emotion. Remember all the solid reasons you listed for dumping her.

Then look around, feast your eyes. What is sauce for the goose is sauce for the gander. There are bound to be plenty of other fit girls with curves right where you like them and glorious kinks you have yet to discover. Work the dancefloor, move around, shake your thing and watch the girls form an orderly queue. (If this does not happen instantly, wait an hour and do it again, when the ladies are a little less choosey).

One word of warning. When you split you may find your best mate moves in on your ex girlfriend and starts tonguing her. She may well reciprocate. Do not be surprised. This is what best mates do. It is a back handed compliment on your taste in women and do not leap to the conclusion they were probably carrying on behind your back before you dumped her. Even if they appear to already have pet names for each other. This is negative thinking. Think positive. Does your best mate have a girlfriend? Is she at the club? Can you move in on her? As Confucius said, '*the best love is love that circulates*', and there is no finer thing two friends can do than swap girlfriends.

At Your Wedding

This is one of the most popular break up scenarios (especially in EastEnders). It is easy to understand why. At the moment when the church organ strikes up that forbidding blast, you may suddenly be overwhelmed by a sense of dread. For those who don't take the sanctity of marriage seriously this feeling may come at the point where the registrar blows his nose and says, 'who's next, can we hurry it along, I've not had me lunch yet'.

Having agreed to her wedding plans simply because it guaranteed a plentiful supply of sex and anyway a wedding takes years to organise, you find yourself being marched up the aisle two weeks later. All of a sudden her family look like gargoyles, especially her cousins with huge biceps and the wonky stares (and that's just the females).

And before your eyes, your fiancé becomes hideously ugly, and the thought of waking up to this woman day after day for the rest of your life fills you with intense displeasure (This feeling shouldn't come until at least two years into a good marriage). If you feel any of these emotions lurking at the back of your mind, it might be a good idea to wear trainers to the ceremony. That way if you change your mind you can leg it.

It will be a very public dumping for her and she may never speak to you for as long as you live, which may not be too much longer if her cousins ever catch up with you, but on the upside she'll be several toasters better off for the experience.

At Someone Else's Wedding

There are always tears at weddings. And not just those of the bride and the bride's mother. Girls are brought up being read fairy tales that always end with the pretty princess getting married to her Prince Charming in a grand, white wedding, with royalty attending the ceremony.

They are read these picture book stories so often it becomes a deep seated longing in them. Even when they grow up to become gorgeous, fit chicks, the little girl in them still wants the fairy-tale ceremony, so much so that any old toad can become a handsome prince in their eyes, if a wedding ceremony is on the cards.

To the bride he is the Prince. To all the other girls present he is an ugly toad. The realisation that their best friend is about to make a huge mistake is enough to make any girl burst into tears. Suddenly they will be wondering, are they too dating a toad? It is in this critical, appraising climate that you can make your move and dump your girlfriend. She may consider herself to have had a lucky escape. Any tears can be explained away as 'joy for her best friend'. You in turn may find the bride up for a pre nuptial fling. Ask. She can only say no.

In Church

Pious girls are hard to dump. No matter how atrocious and ridiculous your behaviour they are inclined to suffer it in the name of God and working on the relationship. Chances are you did not know she was a church girl when you first pulled her. She looked like any other party animal, a true goer. But she has since told you that you are not getting anywhere near the goods till you have pledged yourself to God, received the Priest's blessing and taken Holy Communion.

This is a tough one. You may choose to convert. Many have done so before to receive the earthly pleasures of the flesh. Just ask

---

[4]One other reason a girl will marry a toad, He's RICH!!! Often expressed as, ' he has a nice personality.'

Adam. Others have walked away from the deal. On balance, the better strategy is to be honest with her and true to your firmly held irreligious beliefs. Sit her in a pew and explain that under normal circumstances you could live with being celibate until marriage but as you've only got a few months to live, what is the point?

This revelation may make her question everything she has previously believed in, including a God that would do this to you. At this low ebb and vulnerable, she may give it up. So everyone's a winner.

On Holiday

Holidays are traditionally a time when relationships end. This is because you are forced to spend time together and suddenly all the faults of your partner are highlighted. At least at home you can use work as an excuse not to spend time together but on holiday there is no such luxury, unless you get a part-time job whilst out there.

There's two schools of thought when it comes to breaking up on holiday. A dumping during the holiday could spoil it, what with all the tears and inquests. On the other hand you could both use this new found freedom to bed some locals.

Alternatively you could do the dump on the plane home. This way she is less likely to cause a fuss, what with all the people around. And due to the restrictions on planes, there won't be any sharp implements lying around. That's something to thank terrorists for.

At A Funeral

Funerals are generally similar to weddings, for example it is a time for family gatherings, there are always tears and both indicate a life is over. They also make you think about your own life and make you realise that time is precious and shouldn't be wasted on no hope jobs and girlfriends you don't really fancy. If you dump her straight away it won't add significantly to her grief.

[5] A Legal Notice: If you are sent to Hell, we accept no responsibility.

CHAPTER 5

DUMPING BY CONDUCT

Words sometimes fail us men. Women are often better at using them and don't we know it. Scientists say women's brains are bigger in the language area. This means when it comes to a conversation they can run rings round us and we don't get to say what we mean because we get all confused. To avoid all these difficulties, many men choose to use the dumping by conduct route. It is not cowardice, it is merely playing to our strengths.

If a man is keen on a girl he pays her bills, picks her up anywhere at any time day or night, he loves going shopping with her regardless of how long or how many shops they have to visit and re-visit before she finds that perfect dress. This is because all time spent with her is time in heaven, to the man who is keen.

When in love the man hangs on to his girl's every word, finds sweetness shining from her every pore, even when she asks you to lance the boil on her unwashed big toe, it's all good. Dumping by neglect means cooling off on paying her bills, not wanting to pick her up from the station, making excuses why you cannot go to the Shopping Mall with her and avoiding her feet.

Sound familiar? You are not alone. Statistics prove that ninety six percent of men prefer the neglect method of dumping. But this high percentage is only due to our lack of verbal dexterity. We haven't got the capacity to fully actualise our emotions in verbal forms. Our emotional intelligence is not so finely honed as that of women, indeed we are incapable of tracking the subtle shifts of mood, tone and phrase that is the quintessential ability of a woman at the top of her conversational powers. So we dump by conduct. And we do it well. This chapter will show the following forms of dumping by conduct:

* Get A Dog
* Don't Ring Her
* Suggest A Threesome
* Become An Elvis Impersonator
* Convert To An Annoying Religion
* Pretend You're An Addict
* Grow Spots All Over Your Face
* Start Wearing Slippers and Doing Crosswords.
* Dumping by Doing

Get A Dog

9 out of 10 women prefer cats. They see dogs as farting, slobbering, smelly, demanding, childish creatures, constantly seeking attention and rewards. Dogs are also very much up for sex whatever the occasion and have been known to shag a table leg, just because the table leg gave them 'the eye'.

It's for these reasons dogs remind women of men. To acquire a dog is to outnumber your girlfriend two to one in the household. And since cats and dogs are generally incompatible she cannot even up the odds by bringing home a cat. It is best not to announce the decision to get a dog beforehand. It will only lead to a dialogue consisting primarily of her not agreeing.

Instead bring the dog home straight from the Battered Dogs Home. If it has fleas so much the better. Women hate fleas, and are not even fascinated by the fact they can jump fifty times their own height. If the dog you choose is moulting this is another plus. Moulting dogs rapidly coat all surfaces with a fine layer of smelly hair, leaving her without any free surfaces for depositing false eyelashes, or any of the pots and whatnots that women can't do without.[6]

Howling dogs are 50% more effective at causing a partner to move out than non-howling dogs. If there are no reliable howlers at the kennels get a jumping, yapping dog. This is almost as annoying to her and will threaten her clothes too. If all this fails to get rid of the girlfriend, you may have to take matters into your own hands, urinate in her shoes and blame the dog.

Give it three weeks and nine out of ten girlfriends will be composing their *'I'm leaving you'* speech. The most common

---

[6]For reasons only woman can explain these contraptions are usually spread out all over the bathroom, the living room and the bedroom as opposed to being packed away in the more than adequate make-up bag provided.

form is *'it's me or the dog!'* One thing women should realise is that men don't like ultimatums, so in such circumstances look your girlfriend in the eye and say, *"It was nice knowing you"* Once the dog has served its purpose it's up to you what you decide to do with it. We won't go into too much detail as those animal rights people can be quite dangerous.

Don't Ring Her

Women like to talk more than men. They want, need and expect to be rung at all times, over the most trivial of details such as you crashed her car, had an argument with her mum or accidentally microwaved her cat.

Not only has the mobile phone probably given you brain damage it's also given your girlfriend 24 hour access to your ear. However, with a little bit of cunning we can use this to our advantage.

It is often said 'communication is the key to any successful relationship'. Similarly lack of communication is a major factor when dumping someone: your lack of contact will speak volumes. Ronan Keating summed it up best when he sang "You say it best when you say nothing at all". Please note we don't normally quote Ronan Keating.

The first rule is to avoid actually saying the words, *'I'm dumping you'* instead invent a series of ever more absurd reasons why you did not contact her. Begin with the banal. My phone battery was flat. The network was down. I ran out of credit.

Then move into the territory marked 'more unusual excuses' (the more absurd the better) such as, my mum borrowed my phone, I lost your number and don't have any of your friends' numbers as I find them pretentious. Or I was at the police station, helping them with their enquiries, but as I was really good they wanted me to stay on to try to solve some of their other cases. Or the dog swallowed the phone and I had to cut him open to retrieve it, (extra points for this because as it combines dog with phone, see above). And finally there was a bomb scare and we were told to switch our phones off for 24 hours to avoid activating any hidden bombs. If she actually falls for these far fetched excuses, she's unbelievably stupid and therefore you might want to reconsider dumping her.

It is a matter of pride for many women that they do not do the chasing, so she will expect you to ring her. Her vanity will prevent her from ringing you to find out why you have not rung her. There is a poetic or arithmetic beauty to this situation. You don't ring her. She will not ring you. Result: End of Relationship. Everyone's a winner except possibly the phone companies.

Suggest A Threesome

All men quietly crave a threesome involving their girlfriend plus one of her female friends, who they've mentally assessed as 'worth shagging'.

We don't articulate this desire mainly because we're not stupid, we can anticipate our girlfriend's disgusted reaction to this most simple of requests. If you are at the stage of dumping your girlfriend the threesome suggestion is a win-win scenario for you.

If she gulps at your request but then agrees, you are in for a great steamy night of double helpings, a sex dream come true. You can dump her later, you could even claim that having had sex with this third person, you now realise you can do better. If on the other hand she flounces off calling you a *'filthy minded depraved bastard'* that's good too. She will tell all her friends you split up because you wanted a threesome. They will offer her the much needed shoulder to cry on and the usual platitudes, but girls being girls today don't be surprised if a couple of her friends step forward and offer to sort you out in the threesome department. End Result: Ex girlfriend dumped and a threesome arranged. That's really working your mojo!

Become An Elvis Impersonator

Cool girls want cool boyfriends. A chick likes to look chic when she's out on the town, boyfriend on her arm. If you are pug-ugly, a girl about town will probably agree to a straight forward split proposal. She may have met you at a night club and not realised how ugly you were until taking you home and seeing you in normal light. For the handsome among us, things aren't so easy

splitting up wise. (it's one of the downsides, but we must live with it). We therefore have to uncool ourselves.

Sign up for your local Elvis Appreciation Society. Change the home page on your computer to an Elvis dot com site. Start ordering the Elvis jump suit and shoes from EBay. Start whistling I'm All Shook Up. Sing Jail House Rock in the shower every morning. Has she left yet? If not, take a deep breath, put the clobber on and meet up with her in the middle of town for a night of clubbing. The height of un-coolness is walking down the street dressed up in rhinestones and white spandex while crooning I'm All Shook Up. Take her to the village open mike cabaret and dance up to the stage. Do your hip shaking, microphone rocking best with Blue Suede Shoes. Keep at it.[7] She may wait a few days to see if it is another one of your phases you are going through but any longer and she will be packing her Moschino tops into her Luis Vuitton case and taking to her Jimmy Choos.

Convert To An Annoying Religion

Religion is a great divider and a sure fire relationship splitter. It's also a good excuse to go to war, but that's another matter. If you want to ditch her and don't mind a little worship attendance, adopt

[7]PS. Stop short of dying on the toilet, or working in chip shops.

a religion that will cause her maximum vexation. Ideally you want to find a religion that has as its core rituals car mending, stuffed pizza eating, football match attending (with a special dispensation for watching the World Cup which their top theologian has declared a Holy Period During Which Men Must Have Complete Control Of The TV Remote), porn surfing, drinking beer direct from cans until completely pissed and comatose. This religion must also ban all dancing by males and forbids males accompanying females on shopping expeditions. So far we have been unable to locate such a religion though there is a cult in Leeds that shows promise.

Most mainstream religions have some of the above elements. Several of them give women all the onerous tasks while more or less letting men sit on their fat arses and contemplate the

Universe and other stuff men like to do when the fridge light bulb needs changing or the grass needs cutting.

Pretend you're an addict

Every time you meet up with your girlfriend gargle some whiskey and stuff your pockets with betting slips. This way she will think you are an addict. At some point tell her you are going to go into rehab. She will be relieved you have addressed your problem as no one wants to go out with an addict, except maybe Kate Moss. Tell her not to contact you as it will affect your recovery, re-assure her that you will contact her when you are out.

This will give you some breathing space, at some point she will spot you out and about and she'll want to know why you haven't been in touch. Explain to her that your therapist expressly told you that you must get rid of your past life. For authenticity shave off your hair as this is the accepted symbolic representative of change. If you are already bald, grow a moustache.

Grow Spots All Over Your Face

You may believe that it is the wonders of your personality including your sparkling wit that keeps your girlfriend engaged. You are wrong. As any study will reveal, women don't have much going on in their lives, so when they meet up their main topic of conversation is......us men. And when discussing whether to date or whether to drop a man her and her friends' main consideration is how good looking you are. (Women can be so shallow). If you raise your ugliness factor you increase the chances she will leave you at the earliest opportunity.

Spots are the best turn off. Cultivate exploding pustules close to your mouth so that whenever she goes to kiss you she is repulsed by the sight and smell. Try not washing your face for a week and see if that does the trick. If that fails some have tried puncturing areas of their face with a needle and rubbing dirt in. For legal reasons we don't recommend this but it usually does the job.

Once you have a colony of spots forming, add some TCP or other foul smelling antiseptic. This way if she is a girl who is led by her nose more than her eyes, she will still find you repulsive. Engineer a reason to go out with her and her girl friends. Stay with the group for as long as is polite then wander off. Her girlfriends are bound to tell her just how ugly you are. She will defend you out of pride, but expect a parting of the ways within two weeks on some phoney pretext or other.

_____Start Wearing Slippers and Doing Crosswords

The last thing a girl wants is to be dating her granddad.[8] The following can be done over a number of months in order that she does not think you have suddenly gone mad. Start to wear a badly knitted sweater and start growing a fisherman's bushy beard. Drag in a crusty old armchair from a flea market then sit in it all evening. Develop a hacking cough. Complain the cricket season does not last long enough and what happened to the dancing girls on Top Of The Pops. Start raving about how

Motown vinyl is better than all this new fangled hip hop CD stuff and the hair styles were better back then too. Get a lava lamp to replace the TV. Grow a mullet or a big Afro and wear nylon right down to your underpants. The crackle under the bed sheets will

[8]Nb. This is illegal.

not be flashes of sexual chemistry but the static you generate when you move about. Even the most saintly of girls will flee in a couple of weeks.

Dumping By Doing

This is a more vigorous form of conduct than than any of the above. The best example is shagging other girls and strategically leaving their intimate underwear around your flat so your girlfriend finds them. Strategically in this instance may mean, poking out from a pile of pizza boxes and discarded cans of lager. Following this tactic your girlfriend will not only find out you're a whore, she'll also be disgusted by your untidiness. A double whammy! She will be so ready to leave you!

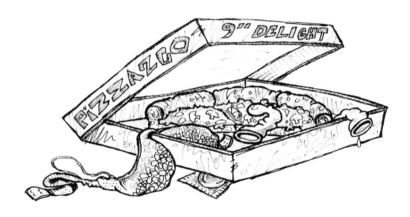

PS. If all else in this section fails, buy as many copies of this book as you can afford and leave them lying around your flat, women are very good at picking up on hints.

Chapter 6

Remote Dumping

Face to face dumping is the most noble method of dumping a girl. But nobility is way out of fashion and you will have achieved little that could not have been achieved by remote dumping (RD). RD delivers accuracy at a distance. RD is not cowardly. It's 21st century. If you don't understand this you are too old and should stop reading this book.

There are pluses and minuses to each way of delivering the 'you're dumped' message to your girlfriend. A little time spent exploring the respective advantages and disadvantages is well worth it. This chapter will look at the following remote dumping methods:

* Texting
* Phones and Phone Messages
* Letters
* On Foot Messengers

Texting

With texts comes power. Start leaving it longer and longer before you reply to her texts. De-personalise your messages, instead of 'Hi Babe' begin your text with 'Alright Mate'. Eventually stop sending her individual texts and just include her in a group text.

If you are going to dump by text, brevity is always best when delivering bad news. *"We need to amputate"* is just one example. When dumping, nothing is briefer than a text message.

Be sure to put an X at the end of the message. It's a nice touch, it basically says, although I'm crapping on you from a great height and never want to see you again, I was once fond of you.

PS. Three XXXs on a dumping txt is just taking the pxxx.

Phones and Phone Messages

It is much easier for couples at war to speak to each other over the phone than face to face. All the little smirks, eyebrow raises and tears trickling down the face (and that's just the men) are not visible and therefore can be ignored. It works on the same principle as, if there is a whole kitchen of dirty dishes, plates, cutlery and stuff you don't even know the names of, and you choose not to see them, then how do you know to wash them up?

What we are trying to say is that the absence of visual signposts helps the conversation run along a more rational and businesslike track. You may extend this business mood by invoicing her for the stuff you have left at her house.

Answering machines are tricky. Talking into a faceless machine is hard when you are sober, and even harder when drunk. There are so many ways in which you can be embarrassed. Without the usual interruptions from the person on the other end of the line ('*I don't believe you. Are you crazy? I will cut your knob off!*') you may stumble, suffer a sudden loss of confidence or plain forget what it was you meant to say. If the chances of getting an answer machine are high, write out a suitable script first and practise it. Pretend it's an award ceremony and you've won, although you don't have to thank God, your parents or your agent anywhere in the message.

Remember she will listen to your message over and over and over again listening to see if there are any clues as to why you're dumping her so it's important you get your words and intonation correct and there are no giggling women in the background.

Be prepared. Have contingency plans in case of the unexpected. What if she picks up? What if her mum picks up midway through your message? Have a script ready for her mum too just in case. Don't dump the daughter then try to date her mum though. It will be far too complicated (just take our word for this).

As we said, the positive aspect of answer machines is you don't get the usual interruptions from the other end of the line, plus it gives you good practice for when phoning to pay your bills or rearrange your debts as you never get to speak to a real person when you dial those 0870 numbers.

Letters

Handwritten letters may be considered quaint but they are also effective and they connect you with a long history of 'I'm ditching you' letters. There is no need to go to the extreme of buying a set of calligraphy pens, this may give the wrong impression. A cheap biro will suffice. Or why not put to good use those pens Oxfam send you in the post?

Writing a handwritten letter will give you a sense of finality. Letters cannot be cut and pasted and infinitely rearranged to suit whichever girl you are about to dump. You will soon tire of rewriting long hand a letter you are unhappy with. Ask yourself: does this letter do the job? If the answer is yes, the letter is good enough. Do not sign the letter using your usual  signature in case you still have joint bank accounts active. Instead sign it off with a grand Edwardian flourish.

Remember to date it for posterity; this will enable her in years to come to look back with confidence as to when this event took place. Putting the date in the corner of the page will also remind you of being back in school as will standing in the corner of a room with your hands on your head.

On Foot Messengers

Go betweens are handy in tough relationship scenarios. They can help keep things calm. And if things don't remain calm, then at least it is the go-between who gets it in the neck rather than yourself. Remember, messengers get shot. Which of your friends would you like to get shot?

Do not send any friend who seems too keen to do the deed for you. They may have ulterior motives. Sending people on your behalf to deliver notes is the old fashioned and some say most romantic way to dump a girl. Henry VIII dumped all his ex's by letter sealed with wax carried by a splendidly attired, hose stockinged, expendable, young courtier. It would be memorable for you to do the same and in later years she might laugh at your panache.

PS. Stop short of Henry VIII's example of beheading some of his exes.

Chapter 7

Finding The Right Words

Many men find it hard to dump their girls because it requires that they put at least three or four sentences together back to back in one go. We have spent a lot of time and effort perfecting the art of running a relationship on grunts, ums, and yeah whatevers. We are not saying you cannot ditch a girl in a series of ums and ahs and grunts. But such a dump rarely as effective as using vocabulary that can actually be found in a dictionary.

Your best tactic on the substance of what you say, is to lie. Your 'official' reason for leaving her should never be contaminated with the truth. This chapter will look at practising whatever you decide you are going to say, and will lookat dry runs and then showcase four effective Dump lies.

* Dry Runs
* I Think I'm Gay
* You Remind Me Too Much Of My Dead Sister
* I Don't Deserve You
* You Don't Deserve Me

Dry Runs

First step find a girl friend to practise with. This girl needn't be a fully RADA trained actress, but she does need to be good at role play (most girls are in our experience). The ideal is someone who looks a bit like your girlfriend, acts a bit like your girlfriend, smells a bit like your girlfriend, – maybe your girlfriend's sister?

This girl will stand in for your girlfriend while you go through your 'you're Dumped' speech. You will gain loads from this dry run. In call-centres they refer to this speech as 'the pitch'. But that's where the similarities end, we don't expect you to move to India to do your dry run.

Ask the stand-in to assume a neutral gaze initially while you go through what you have to say. Then, once you have built up a basic fluency, ask the stand-in to throw in some gestures and verbal responses that your girlfriend might be expected to come up with during the real dump.

When doing a dry run, do consider the setting. The closer you can get to an environment similar to the one where it is going to happen for real, the more useful your dry run will be. Those in the army call this a reccie. But that's where the similarities end, we don't expect you to go to a war torn country to do your dry run.

Beware also of adding too much realism. For instance, if you decide to do a dry run in a crowded local pub, people might overhear and mistake it for the real thing. This misinterpretation may work its way back to your girl and she will accuse you of having been two-timing her. If this happens, you might as well embrace the situation, say yes, you were, and hope she dumps you for the alleged betrayal. This is what is known in game theory as an unexpected beneficial outcome. If you use a pub for your dry run, be sure it isn't the pub your girlfriend's dad drinks in, as this may lead to a different unexpected outcome.

_____**'I Think I'm Gay'**

Sit your soon-to-be ex down, your knees touching her knees, your hands in her lap pressed together, and deliver the line, *'I think I'm gay.'* Let her absorb this and work through the shock for a moment then elaborate. Say you have been fighting these feelings for a long time, that it is no insult to her and you have never actually had any 'man on man' action but that you get these urges: you suddenly find yourself fantasising about what kind of underwear her dad is wearing, or how her brother would look naked and whether he would be up for a spot of olive oil wrestling.

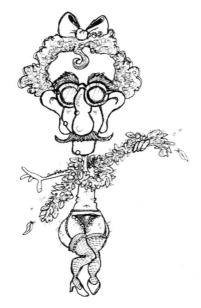

Now boost her self esteem. Say she is the one who has kept you straight for so many weeks or months and she still gives you an erection every time you scent her pussy, but it would be unfair to continue the relationship, you need to explore the urges. Explain away your many other former girlfriends as you being unsure and fickle, you were desperately attempting to find out if any woman had what you wanted sexually. Explain away the smutty naked girls DVDs and subscription to the Playboy Channel as just a cover for when your mates come round.

Once you have dumped her, do NOT be seen immediately dating the girl you have in the wings. This will blow your story. If you really want your story to be accepted as being true, make sure you are seen walking round town, hand in hand with a man, whilst singing show tunes.

For a few weeks after you may find she calls to chat about new guys she is fancying. Keep up your pretence, sound interested and pretend you too could fancy the guy she is dreaming of. This should stop the frequency of these calls.

A couple of months later, when all the dust has settled, say the man on man thing turned out to be a disappointment, you've discovered you don't like hairy-arsed bodies and you are back with girls (though not ones with hairy arses).

_____'You Remind Me Too Much Of My Dead Sister'

This is another favourite. Begin by saying you have never loved a girlfriend more deeply, more totally with all your heart and soul than you have loved her. Your times together have been very special and are the best memories you have ever had in your entire life. Yet, as you became closer and closer you began to understand the attraction you had for her. This attraction is strange and wonderful but unhealthy. Then say the line: *'you remind me in too many ways of my dead sister'* (or other relative, preferably a female one).

Explain you were closer to your sister than to anybody else in the family and that when she passed away your world was shattered. You had not realised it but ever since then you have been seeking her in other people. It is only now you have gone in for counselling that you have learned that this is unhealthy. You have to move on and leave your sister in peace. As part of that, the relationship has to end. Otherwise in your mind, you will be committing incest and although you loved your sister dearly, it was not that kind of love. Promise the ex that she will always be your friend, just as your sister was.

Try to avoid answering too many questions about what your sister looked like, what it was you particularly liked about her, how old she was when she died etc. The beauty of this whole approach is you avoid the flaming rows and instead gain your ex's sympathy. So long as you don't start going out with a girl who looks like the ex, you are on safe ground and it will all hold up. If your brother tells her you don't have a dead sister, just say he's in denial, the whole family is in denial, it's one of the many family skeletons.

'I Don't Deserve You'

Women have very high standard in many things. Just tell her you can't reach her standards in whatever she's most proud of eg being tidy and organised, sex positions etc. Weakness is strength in this approach and let's face it we men have plenty of weaknesses, just ask your girlfriend.

For example if she is tidy and organised, confess you are a messy individual. You admire and aspire to the standards of tidiness that your girlfriend has. You fight with yourself every day to pair up socks and fold underwear and arrange the magazines by date order and use the least fresh milk bottle before the most recent, make love on alternate days, first day in daylight, second at night. But you have to come to terms with the miserable reality. You will never attain her standards of organisation and tidiness.

Far better in these circumstances to part, for you to take some adult learner course in filing and tidying up, join the army where they drill it into you, and then, after a five year break, see if you two can hook up together again. So long as you sort the CDs and clothes into neat His and Hers piles before you leave, she will not suffer too much.

Try to go out with a scruffy girl in baggy unwashed clothes for a while to ward the ex off. These types are often found in and around student unions.

The *I Don't Deserve You* explanation has the beauty of humility. It is another variant on the *'it's not you, it's me'* approach that works so well in situations like these. However there are other possibilities than humility.

'You Don't Deserve Me'

This approach praises and condemns at one and the same time. It goes, *'I had low self esteem, but you've taught me to value myself. Now my self esteem is sorted out, I've decided you are not good enough for me.'*

This has the poetry of logic. She wanted you to believe you could do better in every sphere. You quit your McJob and became a trainee tax accountant. You moved out of the flat your mate let you rent cheap because you had to flush the toilet with a bucket and moved into her wood floor apartment and paid half the rent which was amazingly cheap for such a status symbol even if it was a bit small. You threw out your wardrobe of comfortable clothes and wore dry cleaned white shirts and stiff black suits because it gave you that aspirational look and everyone knows you have to look the part in order to become the part. Now you are a success. You've got a big paying job and the flash car. But you've caught the aspirational bug. You must drive on and up constantly. You've changed everything but the girl. It's now time to change the girl.

She was good for the stage in your life you were at,* but she has taught you to aim higher. But more importantly you now feel you can get a better looking and dirtier in bed girlfriend. It is time to leave her behind along with all the other not good enough bits of your old life. How can she complain? It is everything she told you to do and women love it when men do as they are told.

---

* Dumping someone as your status changes is not unusual, I know I'm dumping my girlfriend if this book takes off. J.D

Final Chapter

Stuff We Couldn't Fit In Elsewhere

A good Dumper is like a good dancer. For both, there is a lot of footwork involved. What we have laid down in the preceding chapters, are the basic foundations – the elementary steps if you like – of how to get it done. Everything you need to know to become a competent dumper is above. In this last chapter we have pulled together some miscellaneous aspects of dumping for those who are really keen on the subject. These are:

* Tactics To Confound Arranged Marriage Set Ups
* Dumping More Than One Girlfriend At A Time
* Pre-emptive dumping
* Decoys
* Reading Your Girlfriend's Body Language
* The Blind Date Dump
* Dumping By Following The Template Of Love

_____Tactics To Confound Arranged Marriage Set Ups

If you are sitting on your bum all day with never the hint of a desire to chase pussy, that's ok with us, we understand the mood. The whole dating lark can be so time consuming and energy sapping. You have to make yourself presentable to the opposite sex, wear those itchy new clothes and change your underwear every day. In addition to this, there are the gifts, the club entry fees and the sky high cost of drinks, especially fancy, girls' drinks. Plus you have to think up the customary lies so she thinks you are someone worth going out with.

It's far easier to chill out in your room at your parents' house and allow mum to provide butlering, chef-ing and maid services, like any good mum loves to, while you play Vice City on the Playstation. It is under these circumstances that parents start to introduce you to girls. It's partly because they are not seeing you doing enough of your own searching and partly because they want their home back.

Just as in the world of work when you're shuffling paper and tapping away at the keyboard whilst not actually doing anything, just to fool the boss, so here, the secret in this situation is to look busy.

Why not do the Internet dating thing? Find a decent matchmaking site and subscribe to it. Then let your parents come into your room and go through the respectable Internet girls with them (not your favourite porn sites). Invite them to express a preference. Then when they have chosen a girl from the site for you, no matter how grotty she is, tell them you will contact her and see. This is the beauty of the Internet. *(Well, one of the beauties of the internet- JD)*

You can contact her and either be SO honest about yourself that she is instantly put off you, or you can explain that you are only contacting her out of parental pressure and ask her to ignore your overtures.

You may even find an ally, a girl willing to pretend she is dating you so you can calm your parents down and she can calm hers. The two of you could wind up as wicked partners, checking out the whole dating scene together while being each other's excuse not to get romantically entangled with anyone else.

You can flirt with each other, hold hands, stare adoringly at each other, laugh at each other's jokes, throw the occasional drink over each other – everything that couples in love do. However, do not at any point kiss this partner (at least not with tongues). If you and your date-buddy play it too convincingly you may end up persuading not only the outside world and all the aunties and uncles but each other that you are a match made in heaven. That would be shooting yourself in the foot.

_____Dumping More Than One Girlfriend At A Time

First of all, congratulations are in order. It is all blokes' dream to have two or three girls on the go. Especially if they each think they are 'the One'.

There are blokes we have heard of, often plumbers[9] who have managed to keep three girls on the go until the day they die and the girlfriends only discover one another at the funeral. This makes for noisy funerals but great legends.

---

[9]This may explain why plumbers keep nipping off when they're supposed to be installing your new bathroom.

More likely one girlfriend starts to come to the fore. She has all the qualities you have been looking for so you start to tire of the others. It's a bit like those variety packs of crisps. No matter how many flavours there are there's always one that you favour. There are of course some flavours that you only contemplate eating when you come home drunk.

Anyway enough talk of crisps. You've decided you need to dump the others. But before you do, think long and hard about this. Weigh up each girl's pros and cons. Try to imagine yourself without one of your girlfriends. Let us suppose for instance, you have a Saturday girl. What will you do on Saturdays without your football loving, shagging in your favourite team kit calling out 'put it away, bury it!' girl? Can you bear life without her? Is your chosen girl willing to learn the secrets of the sweeper system? Only you know the answers to these questions.

Different girls will have different strengths and bring different things to your table. *(like crisps)* Try to make sure you retain the right girl, otherwise you will be kicking yourself for a long time. The following procedures, like vasectomies, are rarely reversible.

Let's Talk Strategy. Does any one girl know of the existence of any other girl? Scientifically most men are perfectly capable of maintaining a relationship with two to five girlfriends at once, allowing each girl to believe she is the only one. (who said we can't multi-task?) Some experts would say you should have put more time and effort on the one girl instead of chasing the others, not us though.

If this ideal situation has been achieved i.e. they don't know about each other, then it simply becomes a matter of choosing which girl to retain and dumping the others. Start with the one you think will be easiest to dump. In our experience it is the one you care about the least. The more you do it the better you will get, until by the 5th dump you'll be addicted and may start ringing people you don't even know just to dump them.

The dumped girls might seek revenge by revealing your double or triple life to the girl you choose not to dump. Neutralise the effect of these revelations by telling the girl you have retained that you have a stalker. Say a woman you have never seen in your life before and certainly never shared a bed with her, lights on or lights off, never mind shagging her every Saturday has invented a relationship. Explain that some people have nasty minds and it is people like this woman that is at the root of all the world's problems.

The tip here is bare faced lies are the most effective lies. They require boldness. They keep things simple and are hard to trace *(you should have seen the lies we had to tell to get this book published)*.

If the dumped ex is relentless, do two things. Firstly get one of your friends to spend 'time' with her. Women are less likely to be vindictive if they are getting some. We did say "less likely". Meanwhile, you should fly off with the retained girlfriend for a week away. This gets you away from the situation. Lavish time and money on the retained girlfriend while on holiday so as to cement her trust in you. There's nothing that says trust to a woman more than a new wardrobe.

If each girl knew about the other prior to the dumping of one, then the situation is trickier. They will be used to competing for your 'time' and will react to the 'Dumped' news by either wooing you or by attacking the other girl. For some unexplained reason they will rarely attack you, the transgressor.

Every man enjoys a good cat fight, especially if the world and his dog knows the women are fighting over him. It's an ego booster. Nevertheless, the cat fight is not useful in this situation. Why? Because you have lost control. Think. You cannot be sure the

woman you intend to keep will win the fight. If you see a cat fight on the cards it may be better to dump by degrees rather than dump absolutely. A 'by degrees' dump, if done properly is carefully managed over a number of months, and will avoid the nightmare cat fight scenario. See the Dumping By Conduct chapter for information on dumping by degrees.

Pre-emptive dumping

Dumping her before she dumps you has a lot going for it. You can salvage some pride from the wreckage that is your relationship by ensuring you are in the driving seat when your relationship sails over the cliff and hits the rocks. You look far cooler having dumped her than having to take the jibes of your mates when she dumps you, and let's be honest, that's what really matters, right?

So what are the signs that says she may be about to dump you? We have put together a core checklist of tell tale signs:

- She keeps leaving crumpled up notes around your flat saying, *"I don't quite know how to tell you this but…"*
- Your friends tell you.
- Her friends tell you.
- The private detective you've hired tells you.
- She no longer talks to you.
- She no longer visits you.
- You keep finding other men in the double bed.

If one or more of these are true, then it's time to implement your pre-emptive dump. Study the tactics in earlier chapters to figure out the best way.

Decoys

Using decoys is a smart way of getting a girl prepared for being dumped. Have a friend and his girlfriend enact a 'dump' scene in your girlfriend's presence. See how she reacts. If she shrugs, and says, 'ah well, shit happens, it's all level vibes to me, they should both get on with their life' this is good news. The chances are she'll simply shrug again when you tell her you are dumping her. Forge ahead with your dumping plans.

If she reacts by going over to your friend's girlfriend and consoling her, criticising your friend and generally getting excited about it, then you will need to tread more cautiously. Either way you have learned something. The beauty of the decoy set up is that, however she reacts, it introduces dumping as a normal end to relationships, an ordinary experience that everyone goes through at one stage or another and part of the rich tapestry of life. If, in the decoy scene, the girl being dumped is entirely reasonable and accepting of the bloke's decision, so much the better, it will plant that attitude in her mind and smooth the way. This is how advertising works. Anyone who has come back from a quick trip to Asda with loads of food they never really wanted will know what we mean.

Reading Your Girlfriend's Body Language

Use the physical closeness of the two of you to capture advance warning of the reaction your 'I'm Leaving You' speech is going to generate. If, when you begin your speech, both her eyebrows zing high up onto the forehead and her mouth pops open and the voice box of her throat wobbles up and down, you can be sure you are dumping a screamer. Try to manoeuvre yourself and her to a

sound-proofed booth then continue.

If on the other hand, her body stiffens and there is reflexive clutching and unclutching of hands accompanied by darting, jagged eye movements, then you have an axe-chucker before you. Do a quick check for dangerous weapons in your immediate environment. For the lucky Dumpers whose opening line merely elicits a cursory flick of one eyebrow, you've got lucky, she's a shrugger: plough on with the whole speech.

Fatalists and bawlers are also easy to spot with some practice: Eyes rolling towards the sky and palms held upwards while the mouth issues sighs, are key signs of a fatalist. Fists clenched, eyes screwed tightly shut and face taut from imminent tears is the tell tale body language of a bawler. Take preventative action according to category using the tips in chapter three.

The Blind Date Dump

There you are all comfortable and single. Your fridge is full of beer, you can watch sports as long as you like, your kitchen sink is piled up with stuff that you'll wash once a month because its more efficient that way, Mum's doing your laundry but anyway you're buying crease free clothes so not too much to worry about on that score. In short, you are happy as Larry.

Then your friends call round and ruin it. You must be lonely, they allege, we'll set you up on a blind date. In vain you tell them there's no need. They persist. At this point the penny drops. You realise this is not about you, it is about them. They have girlfriends and can't live your slobby life because their girlfriends won't allow them. Now they are determined to kill your bachelor pleasures too.

You protest, fight them off. In a big sulk, they all stop seeing you and start whispering behind your back that you are depressed and need medical help. To stop all the rumours, you cave in and submit to their plans. They want to set you up on a blind date. Great. With smart planning you can keep both them and you happy:

Allow them to dress you. Completely. From your Burberry coat right down to your linen boxer shorts. Accept their view that a girl is not attracted to a guy who wears seven day Y fronts and stay-pressed trousers. Yes, these clothes are comfortable for you. Yes, constant washing wastes the earth's resources. Yes, after a while the smell is unnoticeable. Nevertheless, submit. Think of it this way, you are getting new clothes for free.

Let them shave you. A hairy chin is a sign of macho guy, that much is undeniable. Yet some women are not yet ready for a full-on macho guy. Think positive. Having not shaved for so long, your skin will be in peak condition, totally healed from all the nicks and razor bumps that may have prompted you to first lay down your Wilkinson Sword *(this is not a euphemism)*. And shaving as we all know from the adverts will transform you from someone who looks like a vagrant into a smooth, slick guy, who always pull the fittest girls. Give it a go.

Spray mint in your mouth. As Shakespeare wrote in the first draft of his famous poem: 'although a rose by any other name does smell as sweet, yet a mouth that avoids the toothbrush does oft-times reek.' Most honest people will admit they sometimes skip the drudgery of brushing twice a day. And there is something frankly ridiculous about a grown man flossing. The fact remains that women often surreptitiously inspect teeth when considering

whether to kiss a man, and green teeth are a turn off as is odorous breath. Let your friends buy you a brand new toothbrush and get you to swizzle your mouth in mouthwash. Let them scrub your tongue if it makes them happy. Accept their quick dating lessons with good humour. Your mates will insist on issuing a guide to deportment, manners and speech. Just accept it. It will be pretty much like the list below:

-Looking more than twice in any ten seconds period at a woman's breasts is considered rude, especially if she is talking about a matter of some substance. Especially do not gaze too long at the nipple zone.
-Letting your eyes wander up and down another woman in the presence of your date is also rude, no matter how fit the other woman is.
-If the girl asks you to dance, a shuffle from side to side is perfectly acceptable. Do not try any Usher or Saturday Night Fever moves: these look good in your bedroom mirror only *(if you're lucky).*

-Bodily noises should not be shared experiences until say the 2nd date.

-Pay for food or tickets for a film or concert. Negotiating to split the bill or trying to drive the price down in front of her is not an attractive quality.

-Do not suggest a Fantasy Bar as a good place to meet. Just don't.

- The following are 'no's when making conversation: toe nails, football heroes, life cycle of the dung beetle, how to fit a twelve bore exhaust kit to your hatchback, previous girlfriends. Instead talk about her, ask her what happened at work. For some bizarre reason women assume we care about such trivial matters. Keep the bluff going that you do.

Your mates may serve up some other rules like these. Show willing by faithfully reciting them back to your mates, They will be impressed and encouraged. Keep your nerve. Stick with the plan.

However, be aware of Warning Signs: if your friends will not show you a photo of your prospective date; or if they rave on about her personality; or if they praise her intelligence, then you can safely assume that she is dog quiveringly ugly. Do not despair. Do not panic. Stick with the plan.

The Plan involves setting a time, setting a place and choosing clothing to identify each other by. Let her know you'll be meeting her alone not with your mates watching. Say 'privacy leads to intimacy'. She will be impressed by your seriousness and will also come alone.

Disguise your voice during the initial phone conversation or affect a twang. Voice disguise gives you flexibility later on in the Plan.

Arrange a convenient time and place with your blind date. Try to make it somewhere public, during the day time. It is important that this location has throngs of people passing through it.

Agree the time. Agree that you will both wear a certain item of clothing to identify each other by. Try to make sure yours is a hat or a coat. Make sure you arrive early to scout the place out. Find a good spying place, close to where you are meeting up where

you can hover without being noticed. Place your hat or coat in your bag and await the arrival of your blind date. She may be late. Women like to be a little late for these things. Come to think of it women just like to be late.

When she is in position, have a good look at her. If you don't like what you see, (Eg if the girl waiting for you is hideously ugly or your sister's best mate or both) keep the hat or coat in your bag and slip stealthily away from the scene. Phone or text her ten minutes later and say the arrangement is off as you have just reunited with your ex and you're trying to make a go of it again.

If you do like what you see, stick your hat or coat on and approach her. Your mates have won. Your fridge will soon be full of yoghurts and other healthy stuff.

_____Dumping By Following the Template of Love

People generally put a lot of time and effort into hooking up with a potential partner. Yet so little invention goes into the dump, so why don't you just use the same methods when ending a relationship. For example, you could hire a plane with a banner that reads, '*insert name of Girlfriend* YOU'RE DUMPED!!!' Or you could relay a message over the tannoy at a sporting event. Or you could put together a mix CD with songs all themed so when she listens to the songs she will realise she is getting dumped. Possible songs you could have songs and album are:

-   50 Ways to Leave your Lover- Paul Simon
-   Everyday I love you less and less – Kaiser Chiefs
-   I hate you so much –Kelis
-   I'm not in Love – 10cc
-   Good Riddance – Green Day
-   Goodbye my Lover – James Blunt
-   Tainted Love – Soft Cell

You could end the CD on a positive note, with 'Always Look on the Bright Side of Life', but only if you want.

_____Final Notes

That's it. Good luck with it all. If we make enough money from this book we may write a sequel giving some answers to such thorny post split problems as:
-   keeping open the possibility of the occasional shag after the split up

- visiting her mother because you fancy her mum, or her cooking's really good
- going out with the sister of the ex
- how to react when you see her next day, arms around your best friend who you always suspected she'd fancied anyway

and we'll throw in some sample letters, sample text messages and sample phone scripts.

But more likely we'll become professional wasters, hitting the beaches around the world, avoiding our exes and possibly creating a few new ones along the way!